D0915413

78^{00}

Rupert Brooke &
Wilfred Owen

Selected by
George Walter

PHOENIX
POETRY

This edition first published by Phoenix in 2002.

Second impression 2003

Selection © J. M. Dent 2002
Chronology © J. M. Dent 2002

All rights reserved

ISBN: 0 75381 654 7

Typeset by Deltatype Ltd, Birkenhead, Merseyside
Printed in Great Britain by Clays Ltd, St Ives plc

A CIP catalogue reference for this book
is available from the British Library.

The Orion Publishing Group
Orion House
5 Upper St Martin's Lane
London
WC2H 9EA

Contents

Rupert Brooke

Wilfred Owen

Rupert Brooke

The Little Dog's Day

All in the town were still asleep,
When the sun came up with a shout and a leap.
In the lonely streets unseen by man,
A little dog danced. And the day began.

All his life he'd been good, as far as he could,
And the poor little beast had done all that he should.
But this morning he swore, by Odin and Thor
And the Canine Valhalla – he'd stand it no more!

So his prayer he got granted – to do just what he
    wanted,
Prevented by none, for the space of one day.
'Jam incipiebo, sedere facebo,'
In dog-Latin he quoth, *'Euge! sophos! hurray!'*

He fought with the he-dogs, and winked at the she-
    dogs,
A thing that had never been *heard* of before.
'For the stigma of gluttony, I care not a button!' he
Cried, and ate all he could swallow – and more.

He took sinewy lumps from the shins of old frumps,
And mangled the errand-boys – when he could get
    'em.
He shammed furious *rabies*, and bit all the babies,
And followed the cats up the trees, and then ate 'em!

They thought 'twas the devil was holding a revel,
And sent for the parson to drive him away;
For the town never knew such a hullabaloo
As that little dog raised – till the end of that day.

When the blood-red sun had gone burning down,
And the lights were lit in the little town,
Outside, in the gloom of the twilight grey,
The little dog died when he'd had his day.

Seaside

Swiftly out from the friendly lilt of the band,
  The crowd's good laughter, the loved eyes of men,
  I am drawn nightward; I must turn again
Where, down beyond the low untrodden strand,
There curves and glimmers outward to the unknown
  The old unquiet ocean. All the shade
Is rife with magic and movement. I stray alone
Here on the edge of silence, half afraid,

Waiting a sign. In the deep heart of me
The sullen waters swell towards the moon,
And all my tides set seaward.
                              From inland
Leaps a gay fragment of some mocking tune,
That tinkles and laughs and fades along the sand,
And dies between the seawall and the sea.

Failure

Because God put His adamantine fate
  Between my sullen heart and its desire,
I swore that I would burst the Iron Gate,
  Rise up, and curse Him on His throne of fire.
Earth shuddered at my crown of blasphemy,
  But Love was as a flame about my feet;
  Proud up the Golden Stair I strode; and beat
Thrice on the Gate, and entered with a cry —

All the great courts were quiet in the sun,
  And full of vacant echoes: moss had grown
Over the glassy pavement, and begun
  To creep within the dusty council-halls.
An idle wind blew round an empty throne
  And stirred the heavy curtains on the walls.

Sonnet

Oh! Death will find me, long before I tire
  Of watching you; and swing me suddenly
Into the shade and loneliness and mire
  Of the last land! There, waiting patiently,

One day, I think, I'll feel a cool wind blowing,
  See a slow light across the Stygian tide,
And hear the Dead about me stir, unknowing,
  And tremble. And I shall know that you have died,

And watch you, a broad-browed and smiling dream,
  Pass, light as ever, through the lightless host,
Quietly ponder, start, and sway, and gleam –
  Most individual and bewildering ghost! –

And turn, and toss your brown delightful head
Amusedly, among the ancient Dead.

A Channel Passage

The damned ship lurched and slithered. Quiet and
  quick
 My cold gorge rose; the long sea rolled; I knew
I must think hard of something, or be sick;
 And could think hard of only one thing – *you*!
You, you alone could hold my fancy ever!
 And with you memories come, sharp pain, and dole.
Now there's a choice – heartache or tortured liver!
 A sea-sick body, or a you-sick soul!

Do I forget you? Retchings twist and tie me,
 Old meat, good meals, brown gobbets, up I throw.
Do I remember? Acrid return and slimy,
 The sobs and slobber of a last year's woe.
And still the sick ship rolls. 'Tis hard, I tell ye,
To choose 'twixt love and nausea, heart and belly.

Dust

When the white flame in us is gone,
  And we that lost the world's delight
Stiffen in darkness, left alone
  To crumble in our separate night;

When your swift hair is quiet in death,
  And through the lips corruption thrust
Has stilled the labour of my breath —
  When we are dust, when we are dust! —

Not dead, not undesirous yet,
  Still sentient, still unsatisfied,
We'll ride the air, and shine, and flit,
  Around the places where we died,

And dance as dust before the sun,
  And light of foot, and unconfined,
Hurry from road to road, and run
  About the errands of the wind.

And every mote, on earth or air,
  Will speed and gleam, down later days,
And like a secret pilgrim fare
  By eager and invisible ways,

Nor ever rest, nor ever lie,
  Till, beyond thinking, out of view,
One mote of all the dust that's I
  Shall meet one atom that was you.

Then in some garden hushed from wind,
  Warm in a sunset's afterglow,
The lovers in the flowers will find
  A sweet and strange unquiet grow

Upon the peace; and, past desiring,
  So high a beauty in the air,
And such a light, and such a quiring,
  And such a radiant ecstasy there,

They'll know not if it's fire, or dew,
  Or out of earth, or in the height,
Singing, or flame, or scent, or hue,
  Or two that pass, in light, to light,

Out of the garden, higher, higher . . .
  But in that instant they shall learn
The shattering ecstasy of our fire,
  And the weak passionless hearts will burn

And faint in that amazing glow,
  Until the darkness close above;
And they will know – poor fools, they'll know! –
  One moment, what it is to love.

Mummia

As those of old drank mummia
  To fire their limbs of lead,
Making dead kings from Africa
  Stand pandar to their bed;

Drunk on the dead, and medicined
  With spiced imperial dust,
In a short night they reeled to find
  Ten centuries of lust.

So I, from paint, stone, tale, and rhyme,
  Stuffed love's infinity,
And sucked all lovers of all time
  To rarify ecstasy.

Helen's the hair shuts out from me
  Verona's livid skies;
Gypsy the lips I press; and see
  Two Antonys in your eyes.

The unheard invisible lovely dead
  Lie with us in this place,
And ghostly hands above my head
  Close face to straining face;

Their blood is wine along our limbs;
  Their whispering voices wreathe
Savage forgotten drowsy hymns
  Under the names we breathe;

Woven from their tomb, and one with it,
  The night wherein we press;
Their thousand pitchy pyres have lit
  Your flaming nakedness.

For the uttermost years have cried and clung
  To kiss your mouth to mine;
And hair long dust was caught, was flung,
  Hand shaken to hand divine,

And Life has fired, and Death not shaded,
  All Time's uncounted bliss,
And the height o' the world has flamed and faded, –
  Love, that our love be this!

The Fish

In a cool curving world he lies
And ripples with dark ecstasies.
The kind luxurious lapse and steal
Shapes all his universe to feel
And know and be; the clinging stream
Closes his memory, glooms his dream,
Who lips the roots o' the shore, and glides
Superb on unreturning tides.
Those silent waters weave for him
A fluctuant mutable world and dim,
Where wavering masses bulge and gape
Mysterious, and shape to shape
Dies momently through whorl and hollow,
And form and line and solid follow
Solid and line and form to dream
Fantastic down the eternal stream;
An obscure world, a shifting world,
Bulbous, or pulled to thin, or curled,
Or serpentine, or driving arrows,
Or serene slidings, or March narrows.
There slipping wave and shore are one,
And weed and mud. No ray of sun,
But glow to glow fades down the deep
(As dream to unknown dream in sleep);
Shaken translucency illumes
The hyaline of drifting glooms;
The strange soft-handed depth subdues
Drowned colour there, but black to hues,
As death to living, decomposes –
Red darkness of the heart of roses,
Blue brilliant from dead starless skies,

And gold that lies behind the eyes,
The unknown unnameable sightless white
That is the essential flame of night,
Lustreless purple, hooded green,
The myriad hues that lie between
Darkness and darkness! . . .

                  And all's one.
Gentle, embracing, quiet, dun,
The world he rests in, world he knows,
Perpetual curving. Only – grows
An eddy in that ordered falling,
A knowledge from the gloom, a calling
Weed in the wave, gleam in the mud –
The dark fire leaps along his blood;
Dateless and deathless, blind and still,
The intricate impulse works its will;
His woven world drops back; and he,
Sans providence, sans memory,
Unconscious and directly driven,
Fades to some dank sufficient heaven.

O world of lips, O world of laughter,
Where hope is fleet and thought flies after,
Of lights in the clear night, of cries
That drift along the wave and rise
Thin to the glittering stars above,
You know the hands, the eyes of love!
The strife of limbs, the sightless clinging,
The infinite distance, and the singing
Blown by the wind, a flame of sound,
The gleam, the flowers, and vast around
The horizon, and the heights above –
You know the sigh, the song of love!

But there the night is close, and there
Darkness is cold and strange and bare;
And the secret deeps are whisperless;
And rhythm is all deliciousness;
And joy is in the throbbing tide,
Whose intricate fingers beat and glide
In felt bewildering harmonies
Of trembling touch; and music is
The exquisite knocking of the blood.
Space is no more, under the mud;
His bliss is older than the sun.
Silent and straight the waters run.
The lights, the cries, the willows dim,
And the dark tide are one with him.

Menelaus and Helen

I

Hot through Troy's ruin Menelaus broke
  To Priam's palace, sword in hand, to sate
  On that adulterous whore a ten years' hate
And a king's honour. Through red death, and smoke,
And cries, and then by quieter ways he strode,
  Till the still innermost chamber fronted him.
  He swung his sword, and crashed into the dim
Luxurious bower, flaming like a god.

High sat white Helen, lonely and serene.
  He had not remembered that she was so fair,
And that her neck curved down in such a way;
And he felt tired. He flung the sword away,
  And kissed her feet, and knelt before her there,
The perfect Knight before the perfect Queen.

II

So far the poet. How should he behold
  That journey home, the long connubial years?
  He does not tell you how white Helen bears
Child on legitimate child, becomes a scold,
Haggard with virtue. Menelaus bold
  Waxed garrulous, and sacked a hundred Troys
  'Twixt noon and supper. And her golden voice
Got shrill as he grew deafer. And both were old.

Often he wonders why on earth he went
  Troyward, or why poor Paris ever came.
Oft she weeps, gummy-eyed and impotent;
  Her dry shanks twitch at Paris' mumbled name.
So Menelaus nagged; and Helen cried;
And Paris slept on by Scamander side.

Lust

How should I know? The enormous wheels of will
  Drove me cold-eyed on tired and sleepless feet.
Night was void arms and you a phantom still,
  And day your far light swaying down the street.
As never fool for love, I starved for you;
  My throat was dry and my eyes hot to see.
Your mouth so lying was most heaven in view,
  And your remembered smell most agony.

Love wakens love! I felt your hot wrist shiver
  And suddenly the mad victory I planned
    Flashed real, in your burning bending head . . . .
My conqueror's blood was cool as a deep river
  In shadow; and my heart beneath your hand
    Quieter than a dead man on a bed.

Jealousy

When I see you, who were so wise and cool,
Gazing with silly sickness on that fool
You've given your love to, your adoring hands
Touch his so intimately that each understands,
I know, most hidden things; and when I know
Your holiest dreams yield to the stupid bow
Of his red lips, and that the empty grace
Of those strong legs and arms, that rosy face,
Has beaten your heart to such a flame of love,
That you have given him every touch and move,
Wrinkle and secret of you, all your life,
– Oh! then I know I'm waiting, lover-wife,
For the great time when love is at a close,
And all its fruit's to watch the thickening nose
And sweaty neck and dulling face and eye,
That are yours, and you, most surely, till you die!
Day after day you'll sit with him and note
The greasier tie, the dingy wrinkling coat;
As prettiness turns to pomp, and strength to fat,
And love, love, love to habit!

                              And after that,
When all that's fine in man is at an end,
And you, that loved young life and clean, must tend
A foul sick fumbling dribbling body and old,
When his rare lips hang flabby and can't hold
Slobber, and you're enduring that worst thing,
Senility's queasy furtive love-making,
And searching those dear eyes for human meaning,
Propping the bald and helpless head, and cleaning
A scrap that life's flung by, and love's forgotten, –
Then you'll be tired; and passion dead and rotten;

And he'll be dirty, dirty!

                    O lithe and free

And lightfoot, that the poor heart cries to see,

That's how I'll see your man and you! —

                            But you

— Oh, when *that* time comes, you'll be dirty too!

Dining-Room Tea

When you were there, and you, and you,
Happiness crowned the night; I too,
Laughing and looking, one of all,
I watched the quivering lamplight fall
On plate and flowers and pouring tea
And cup and cloth; and they and we
Flung all the dancing moments by
With jest and glitter. Lip and eye
Flashed on the glory, shone and cried,
Improvident, unmemoried;
And fitfully and like a flame
The light of laughter went and came.
Proud in their careless transience moved
The changing faces that I loved.

Till suddenly, and otherwhence,
I looked upon your innocence.
For lifted clear and still and strange
From the dark woven flow of change
Under a vast and starless sky
I saw the immortal moment lie.
One instant I, an instant, knew
As God knows all. And it and you
I, above Time, oh, blind! could see
In witless immortality.
I saw the marble cup; the tea,
Hung on the air, an amber stream;
I saw the fire's unglittering gleam,
The painted flame, the frozen smoke.
No more the flooding lamplight broke
On flying eyes and lips and hair;

But lay, but slept unbroken there,
On stiller flesh, and body breathless,
And lips and laughter stayed and deathless,
And words on which no silence grew.
Light was more alive than you.

For suddenly, and otherwhence,
I looked on your magnificence.
I saw the stillness and the light,
And you, august, immortal, white,
Holy and strange; and every glint
Posture and jest and thought and tint
Freed from the mask of transiency,
Triumphant in eternity,
Immote, immortal.

        Dazed at length
Human eyes grew, mortal strength
Wearied; and Time began to creep.
Change closed about me like a sleep.
Light glinted on the eyes I loved.
The cup was filled. The bodies moved.
The drifting petal came to ground.
The laughter chimed its perfect round.
The broken syllable was ended.
And I, so certain and so friended,
How could I cloud, or how distress,
The heaven of your unconsciousness?
Or shake at Time's sufficient spell,
Stammering of lights unutterable?
The eternal holiness of you,
The timeless end, you never knew,
The peace that lay, the light that shone.
You never knew that I had gone

A million miles away, and stayed
A million years. The laughter played
Unbroken round me; and the jest
Flashed on. And we that knew the best
Down wonderful hours grew happier yet.
I sang at heart, and talked, and eat,
And lived from laugh to laugh, I too,
When you were there, and you, and you.

The Old Vicarage, Grantchester

(*Café des Westens*, Berlin, May 1912)

Just now the lilac is in bloom,
All before my little room;
And in my flower-beds, I think,
Smile the carnation and the pink;
And down the borders, well I know,
The poppy and the pansy blow . . .
Oh! there the chestnuts, summer through,
Beside the river make for you
A tunnel of green gloom, and sleep
Deeply above; and green and deep
The stream mysterious glides beneath,
Green as a dream and deep as death.
– Oh, damn! I know it! and I know
How the May fields all golden show,
And when the day is young and sweet,
Gild gloriously the bare feet
That run to bathe . . .
                              Du lieber Gott!

Here am I, sweating, sick, and hot,
And there the shadowed waters fresh
Lean up to embrace the naked flesh.
Temperamentvoll German Jews
Drink beer around; – and *there* the dews
Are soft beneath a morn of gold.
Here tulips bloom as they are told;
Unkempt about those hedges blows
An English unofficial rose;
And there the unregulated sun

Slopes down to rest when day is done,
And wakes a vague unpunctual star,
A slippered Hesper; and there are
Meads towards Haslingfield and Coton
Where *das Betreten*'s not *verboten*.

εἴθε γενοίμην . . . would I were
In Grantchester, in Grantchester! —
Some, it may be, can get in touch
With Nature there, or Earth, or such.
And clever modern men have seen
A Faun a-peeping through the green,
And felt the Classics were not dead,
To glimpse a Naiad's reedy head,
Or hear the Goat-foot piping low: . . .
But these are things I do not know.
I only know that you may lie
Day long and watch the Cambridge sky,
And, flower-lulled in sleepy grass,
Hear the cool lapse of hours pass,
Until the centuries blend and blur
In Grantchester, in Grantchester. . . .
Still in the dawnlit waters cool
His ghostly Lordship swims his pool,
And tries the strokes, essays the tricks,
Long learnt on Hellespont, or Styx.
Dan Chaucer hears his river still
Chatter beneath a phantom mill.
Tennyson notes, with studious eye,
How Cambridge waters hurry by . . .
And in that garden, black and white,
Creep whispers through the grass all night;
And spectral dance, before the dawn,
A hundred Vicars down the lawn;

Curates, long dust, will come and go
On lissom, clerical, printless toe;
And oft between the boughs is seen
The sly shade of a Rural Dean . . .
Till, at a shiver in the skies,
Vanishing with Satanic cries,
The prim ecclesiastic rout
Leaves but a startled sleeper-out,
Grey heavens, the first bird's drowsy calls,
The falling house that never falls.

God! I will pack, and take a train,
And get me to England once again!
For England's the one land, I know,
Where men with Splendid Hearts may go;
And Cambridgeshire, of all England,
The shire for Men who Understand;
And of that district I prefer
The lovely hamlet Grantchester.
For Cambridge people rarely smile,
Being urban, squat, and packed with guile;
And Royston men in the far South
Are black and fierce and strange of mouth;
At Over they fling oaths at one,
And worse than oaths at Trumpington,
And Ditton girls are mean and dirty,
And there's none in Harston under thirty,
And folks in Shelford and those parts
Have twisted lips and twisted hearts,
And Barton men make Cockney rhymes,
And Coton's full of nameless crimes,
And things are done you'd not believe
At Madingley, on Christmas Eve.
Strong men have run for miles and miles,

When one from Cherry Hinton smiles;
Strong men have blanched, and shot their wives,
Rather than send them to St Ives;
Strong men have cried like babes, bydam,
To hear what happened at Babraham.
But Grantchester! ah, Grantchester!
There's peace and holy quiet there,
Great clouds along pacific skies,
And men and women with straight eyes,
Lithe children lovelier than a dream,
A bosky wood, a slumbrous stream,
And little kindly winds that creep
Round twilight corners, half asleep.
In Grantchester their skins are white;
They bathe by day, they bathe by night;
The women there do all they ought;
The men observe the Rules of Thought.
They love the Good; they worship Truth;
They laugh uproariously in youth;
(And when they get to feeling old,
They up and shoot themselves, I'm told) . . .

    Ah God! to see the branches stir
Across the moon at Grantchester!
To smell the thrilling-sweet and rotten
Unforgettable, unforgotten
River-smell, and hear the breeze
Sobbing in the little trees.
Say, do the elm-clumps greatly stand
Still guardians of that holy land?
The chestnuts shade, in reverend dream,
The yet unacademic stream?
Is dawn a secret shy and cold
Anadyomene, silver-gold?

And sunset still a golden sea
From Haslingfield to Madingley?
And after, ere the night is born,
Do hares come out about the corn?
Oh, is the water sweet and cool,
Gentle and brown, above the pool?
And laughs the immortal river still
Under the mill, under the mill?
Say, is there Beauty yet to find?
And Certainty? and Quiet kind?
Deep meadows yet, for to forget
The lies, and truths, and pain? . . . oh! yet
Stands the Church clock at ten to three?
And is there honey still for tea?

Love

Love is a breach in the walls, a broken gate,
  Where that comes in that shall not go again;
Love sells the proud heart's citadel to Fate.
  They have known shame, who love unloved. Even
    then
When two mouths, thirsty each for each, find slaking,
  And agony's forgot, and hushed the crying
Of credulous hearts, in heaven – such are but taking
  Their own poor dreams within their arms, and lying
Each in his lonely night, each with a ghost.
  Some share that night. But they know, love grows
    colder,
Grows false and dull, that was sweet lies at most.
  Astonishment is no more in hand or shoulder,
But darkens, and dies out from kiss to kiss.
All this is love; and all love is but this.

It's Not Going to Happen Again

I have known the most dear that is granted us here
  More supreme than the gods know above,
Like a star I was hurled throught the sweet of the
    world,
  And the height and the light of it, Love.
I have risen to the uttermost Heaven of Joy,
  I have sunk to the sheer Hell of Pain —
But — it's not going to happen again, my boy,
  It's not going to happen again.

It's the very first word that poor Juliet heard
  From her Romeo over the Styx;
And the Roman will tell Cleopatra in hell
  When she starts the immortal old tricks;
What Paris was tellin' for good-bye to Helen
  As he bundled her into the train —
Oh, it's not going to happen again, old girl,
  It's not going to happen again.

There's Wisdom in Women

'Oh love is fair, and love is rare;' my dear one she
    said,
'But love goes lightly over.' I bowed her foolish head,
And kissed her hair and laughed at her. Such a child
    was she;
So new to love, so true to love, and she spoke so
    bitterly.

But there's wisdom in women, of more than they have
    known,
And thoughts go blowing through them, are wiser than
    their own,
Or how should my dear one, being ignorant and
    young,
Have cried on love so bitterly, with so true a tongue?

Clouds

Down the blue night the unending columns press
　In noiseless tumult, break and wave and flow,
　Now tread the far South, or lift rounds of snow
Up to the white moon's hidden loveliness.
Some pause in their grave wandering comradeless,
　And turn with profound gesture vague and slow,
　As who would pray good for the world, but know
Their benediction empty as they bless.

They say that the Dead die not, but remain
　Near to the rich heirs of their grief and mirth.
　　I think they ride the calm mid-heaven, as these,
In wise majestic melancholy train,
　　And watch the moon, and the still-raging seas,
　And men, coming and going on the earth.

A Memory (From a sonnet-sequence)

Somewhile before the dawn I rose, and stept
  Softly along the dim way to your room,
  And found you sleeping in the quiet gloom,
And holiness about you as you slept.
I knelt there; till your waking fingers crept
  About my head, and held it. I had rest
  Unhoped this side of Heaven, beneath your breast.
I knelt a long time, still; nor even wept.

It was great wrong you did me; and for gain
Of that poor moment's kindliness, and ease,
And sleepy mother-comfort!
                                        Child, you know
How easily love leaps out to dreams like these,
Who has seen them true. And love that's wakened so
Takes all too long to lay asleep again.

Heaven

Fish (fly-replete, in depth of June,
Dawdling away their wat'ry noon)
Ponder deep wisdom, dark or clear,
Each secret fishy hope or fear.
Fish say, they have their Stream and Pond;
But is there anything Beyond?
This life cannot be All, they swear,
For how unpleasant, if it were!
One may not doubt that, somehow, Good
Shall come of Water and of Mud;
And, sure, the reverent eye must see
A Purpose in Liquidity.
We darkly know, by Faith we cry,
The future is not Wholly Dry.
Mud unto mud! – Death eddies near –
Not here the appointed End, not here!
But somewhere, beyond Space and Time,
Is wetter water, slimier slime!
And there (they trust) there swimmeth One
Who swam ere rivers were begun,
Immense, of fishy form and mind,
Squamous, omnipotent, and kind;
And under that Almighty Fin,
The littlest fish may enter in.
Oh! never fly conceals a hook,
Fish say, in the Eternal Brook,
But more than mundane weeds are there,
And mud, celestially fair;
Fat caterpillars drift around,
And Paradisal grubs are found;
Unfading moths, immortal flies,

And the worm that never dies.
And in that Heaven of all their wish,
There shall be no more land, say fish.

One Day

Today I have been happy. All the day
  I held the memory of you, and wove
Its laughter with the dancing light o' the spray,
  And sowed the sky with tiny clouds of love,
And sent you following the white waves of sea,
  And crowned your head with fancies, nothing worth,
Stray buds from that old dust of misery,
  Being glad with a new foolish quiet mirth.

So lightly I played with those dark memories,
Just as a child, beneath the summer skies,
  Plays hour by hour with a strange shining stone,
For which (he knows not) towns were fire of old,
  And love has been betrayed, and murder done,
And great kings turned to a little bitter mould.

Hauntings

In the grey tumult of these after years
  Oft silence falls; the incessant wranglers part;
And less-than-echoes of remembered tears
  Hush all the loud confusion of the heart;
And a shade, through the toss'd ranks of mirth and
    crying
  Hungers, and pains, and each dull passionate mood, –
Quite lost, and all but all forgot, undying,
  Comes back the ecstasy of your quietude.

So a poor ghost, beside his misty streams,
Is haunted by strange doubts, evasive dreams,
  Hints of a pre-Lethean life, of men,
Stars, rocks, and flesh, things unintelligible,
  And light on waving grass, he knows not when,
And feet that ran, but where, he cannot tell.

Fafaïa

Stars that seem so close and bright,
Watched by lovers through the night,
Swim in emptiness, men say,
Many a mile and year away.

And yonder star that burns so white,
May have died to dust and night
Ten, maybe, or fifteen year,
Before it shines upon my dear.

Oh! often among men below,
Heart cries out to heart, I know,
And one is dust a many years,
Child, before the other hears.

Heart from heart is all as far,
Fafaïa, as star from star.

The Great Lover

I have been so great a lover: filled my days
So proudly with the splendour of Love's praise,
The pain, the calm, and the astonishment,
Desire illimitable, and still content,
And all dear names men use, to cheat despair,
For the perplexed and viewless streams that bear
Our hearts at random down the dark of life.
Now, ere the unthinking silence on that strife
Steals down, I would cheat drowsy Death so far,
My night shall be remembered for a star
That outshone all the suns of all men's days.
Shall I not crown them with immortal praise
Whom I have loved, who have given me, dared with
    me
High secrets, and in darkness knelt to see
The inenarrable godhead of delight?
Love is a flame: — we have beaconed the world's night.
A city: — and we have built it, these and I.
An emperor: — we have taught the world to die.
So, for their sakes I loved, ere I go hence,
And the high cause of Love's magnificence,
And to keep loyalties young, I'll write those names
Golden for ever, eagles, crying flames,
And set them as a banner, that men may know,
To dare the generations, burn, and blow
Out on the wind of Time, shining and streaming. . . .

These I have loved:
                    White plates and cups, clean-gleaming,
Ringed with blue lines; and feathery, faery dust;
Wet roofs, beneath the lamp-light; the strong crust

Of friendly bread; and many-tasting food;
Rainbows; and the blue bitter smoke of wood;
And radiant raindrops couching in cool flowers;
And flowers themselves, that sway through sunny
    hours,
Dreaming of moths that drink them under the moon;
Then, the cool kindliness of sheets, that soon
Smooth away trouble; and the rough male kiss
Of blankets; grainy wood; live hair that is
Shining and free; blue-massing clouds; the keen
Unpassioned beauty of a great machine;
The benison of hot water; furs to touch;
The good smell of old clothes; and other such –
The comfortable smell of friendly fingers,
Hair's fragrance, and the musty reek that lingers
About dead leaves and last year's ferns. . . .

                                    Dear names,
And thousand other throng to me! Royal flames;
Sweet water's dimpling laugh from tap or spring;
Holes in the ground; and voices that do sing;
Voices in laughter, too; and body's pain,
Soon turned to peace; and the deep-panting train;
Firm sands; the little dulling edge of foam
That browns and dwindles as the wave goes home;
And washen stones, gay for an hour; the cold
Graveness of iron; moist black earthen mould;
Sleep; and high places; footprints in the dew;
And oaks; and brown horse-chestnuts, glossy-new;
And new-peeled sticks; and shining pools on grass; –
All these have been my loves. And these shall pass,
Whatever passes not, in the great hour,
Nor all my passion, all my prayers, have power
To hold them with me through the gate of Death.
They'll play deserter, turn with the traitor breath,

Break the high bond we made, and sell Love's trust
And sacramented covenant to the dust.
—Oh, never a doubt but, somewhere, I shall wake,
And give what's left of love again, and make
New friends, now strangers. . . .

                                    But the best I've known,
Stays here, and changes, breaks, grows old, is blown
About the winds of the world, and fades from brains
Of living men, and dies.

                        Nothing remains.

O dear my loves, O faithless, once again
This one last gift I give: that after men
Shall know, and later lovers, far-removed,
Praise you, 'All these were lovely'; say, 'He loved.'

Retrospect

In your arms was still delight,
Quiet as a street at night;
And thoughts of you, I do remember,
Were green leaves in a darkened chamber,
Were dark clouds in a moonless sky.
Love, in you, went passing by,
Penetrative, remote, and rare,
Like a bird in the wide air,
And, as the bird, it left no trace
In the heaven of your face.
In your stupidity I found
The sweet hush after a sweet sound.
All about you was the light
That dims the greying end of night;
Desire was the unrisen sun,
Joy the day not yet begun,
With tree whispering to tree,
Without wind, quietly.
Wisdom slept within your hair,
And Long-Suffering was there,
And, in the flowing of your dress,
Undiscerning Tenderness.
And when you thought, it seemed to me,
Infinitely, and like a sea,
About the slight world you had known
Your vast unconsciousness was thrown. . . .

O haven without wave or tide!
Silence, in which all songs have died!
Holy book, where hearts are still!
And home at length under the hill!

O mother quiet, breasts of peace,
Where love itself would faint and cease!
O infinite deep I never knew,
I would come back, come back to you,
Find you, as a pool unstirred,
Kneel down by you, and never a word,
Lay my head, and nothing said,
In your hands, ungarlanded;
And a long watch you would keep;
And I should sleep, and I should sleep!

Tiare Tahiti

Mamua, when our laughter ends,
And hearts and bodies, brown as white,
Are dust about the doors of friends,
Or scent ablowing down the night,
Then, oh! then, the wise agree,
Comes our immortality.
Mamua, there waits a land
Hard for us to understand.
Out of time, beyond the sun,
All are one in Paradise,
You and Pupure are one,
And Taü, and the ungainly wise.
There the Eternals are, and there
The Good, the Lovely, and the True,
And Types, whose earthly copies were
The foolish broken things we knew;
There is the Face, whose ghosts we are;
The real, the never-setting Star;
And the Flower, of which we love
Faint and fading shadows here;
Never a tear, but only Grief;
Dance, but not the limbs that move;
Songs in Song shall disappear;
Instead of lovers, Love shall be;
For hearts, Immutability;
And there, on the Ideal Reef,
Thunders the Everlasting Sea!

 And my laughter, and my pain,
Shall home to the Eternal Brain.
And all lovely things, they say,
Meet in Loveliness again;

Miri's laugh, Teïpo's feet,
And the hands of Matua,
Stars and sunlight there shall meet
Coral's hues and rainbows there,
And Teüra's braided hair;
And with the starred *tiare's* white,
And white birds in the dark ravine,
And *flamboyants* ablaze at night,
And jewels, and evening's after-green,
And dawns of pearl and gold and red,
Mamua, your lovelier head!
And there'll no more be one who dreams
Under the ferns, of crumbling stuff,
Eyes of illusion, mouth that seems,
All time-entangled human love.
And you'll no longer swing and sway
Divinely down the scented shade,
Where feet to Ambulation fade,
And moons are lost in endless Day.
How shall we wind these wreaths of ours,
Where there are neither heads nor flowers?
Oh, Heaven's Heaven! – but we'll be missing
The palms, and sunlight, and the south;
And there's an end, I think, of kissing,
When our mouths are one with Mouth. . . .

   Taü here, Mamua,
Crown the hair, and come away!
Hear the calling of the moon,
And the whispering scents that stray
About the idle warm lagoon.
Hasten, hand in human hand,
Down the dark, the flowered way,
Along the whiteness of the sand,

And in the water's soft caress,
Wash the mind of foolishness,
Mamua, until the day.
Spend the glittering moonlight there
Pursuing down the soundless deep
Limbs that gleam and shadowy hair,
Or floating lazy, half-asleep.
Dive and double and follow after,
Snare in flowers, and kiss, and call,
With lips that fade, and human laughter
And faces individual,
Well this side of Paradise! . . .
    There's little comfort in the wise.

The Treasure

When colour goes home into the eyes,
  And lights that shine are shut again
With dancing girls and sweet birds' cries
  Behind the gateways of the brain;
And that no-place which gave them birth, shall close
The rainbow and the rose:–

Still may Time hold some golden space
  Where I'll unpack that scented store
Of song and flower and sky and face,
  And count, and touch, and turn them o'er,
Musing upon them; as a mother, who
Has watched her children all the rich day through,
Sits, quiet-handed, in the fading light,
When children sleep, ere night.

1914

I. Peace

Now, God be thanked Who has matched us with His
  hour,
  And caught our youth, and wakened us from
  sleeping,
With hand made sure, clear eye, and sharpened power,
  To turn, as swimmers into cleanness leaping,
Glad from a world grown old and cold and weary,
  Leave the sick hearts that honour could not move,
And half-men, and their dirty songs and dreary,
  And all the little emptiness of love!

Oh! we, who have known shame, we have found
  release there,
  Where there's no ill, no grief, but sleep has mending,
  Naught broken save this body, lost but breath;
Nothing to shake the laughing heart's long peace there
  But only agony, and that has ending;
  And the worst friend and enemy is but Death.

II. Safety

Dear! of all happy in the hour, most blest
   He who has found our hid security,
Assured in the dark tides of the world that rest,
   And heard our word, 'Who is so safe as we?'
We have found safety with all things undying,
   The winds, and morning, tears of men and mirth,
The deep night, and birds singing, and clouds flying,
   And sleep, and freedom, and the autumnal earth.
We have built a house that is not for Time's throwing.
   We have gained a peace unshaken by pain for ever.
War knows no power. Safe shall be my going,
   Secretly armed against all death's endeavour;
Safe though all safety's lost; safe where men fall;
And if these poor limbs die, safest of all.

III. The Dead

Blow out, you bugles, over the rich Dead!
  There's none of these so lonely and poor of old,
  But, dying, has made us rarer gifts than gold.
These laid the world away; poured out the red
Sweet wine of youth; gave up the years to be
  Of work and joy, and that unhoped serene,
  That men call age; and those who would have been,
Their sons, they gave, their immortality.

Blow, bugles, blow! They brought us, for our dearth,
  Holiness, lacked so long, and Love, and Pain.
Honour has come back, as a king, to earth,
  And paid his subjects with a royal wage;
And Nobleness walks in our ways again;
  And we have come into our heritage.

IV. The Dead

These hearts were woven of human joys and cares,
  Washed marvellously with sorrow, swift to mirth.
The years had given them kindness. Dawn was theirs,
  And sunset, and the colours of the earth.
These had seen movement, and heard music; known
  Slumber and waking; loved; gone proudly friended;
Felt the quick stir of wonder; sat alone;
    Touched flowers and furs and cheeks. All this is
      ended.

There are waters blown by changing winds to laughter
And lit by the rich skies, all day. And after,
  Frost, with a gesture, stays the waves that dance
And wandering loveliness. He leaves a white
  Unbroken glory, a gathered radiance,
A width, a shining peace, under the night.

V. The Soldier

If I should die, think only this of me:
  That there's some corner of a foreign field
That is for ever England. There shall be
  In that rich earth a richer dust concealed;
A dust whom England bore, shaped, made aware,
  Gave, once, her flowers to love, her ways to roam,
A body of England's, breathing English air,
  Washed by the rivers, blest by suns of home.

And think, this heart, all evil shed away,
  A pulse in the eternal mind, no less
    Gives somewhere back the thoughts by England
      given;
Her sights and sounds; dreams happy as her day;
  And laughter, learnt of friends; and gentleness,
    In hearts at peace, under an English heaven.

Fragment

I strayed about the deck, an hour, tonight
Under a cloudy moonless sky; and peeped
In at the windows, watched my friends at table,
Or playing cards, or standing in the doorway,
Or coming out into the darkness. Still
No one could see me.

              I would have thought of them
– Heedless, within a week of battle – in pity,
Pride in their strength and in the weight and firmness
And link'd beauty of bodies, and pity that
This gay machine of splendour 'ld soon be broken,
Thought little of, pashed, scattered. . . .

                Only, always,
I could but see them – against the lamplight – pass
Like coloured shadows, thinner than filmy glass,
Slight bubbles, fainter than the wave's faint light,
That broke to phosphorus out in the night,
Perishing things and strange ghosts – soon to die
To other ghosts – this one, or that, or I.

Wilfred Owen

Anthem for Doomed Youth

What passing-bells for these who die as cattle?
　　Only the monstrous anger of the guns.
　　Only the stuttering rifles' rapid rattle
Can patter out their hasty orisons.
No mockeries for them; no prayers nor bells,
Nor any voice of mourning save the choirs, –
The shrill, demented choirs of wailing shells;
And bugles calling for them from sad shires.

What candles may be held to speed them all?
　　Not in the hands of boys, but in their eyes
Shall shine the holy glimmers of goodbyes.
　　The pallor of girls' brows shall be their pall;
Their flowers the tenderness of patient minds,
And each slow dusk a drawing-down of blinds.

The Unreturning

Suddenly night crushed out the day and hurled
Her remnants over cloud-peaks, thunder-walled.
Then fell a stillness such as harks appalled
When far-gone dead return upon the world.

There watched I for the Dead; but no ghost woke.
Each one whom Life exiled I named and called.
But they were all too far, or dumbed, or thralled;
And never one fared back to me or spoke.

Then peered the indefinite unshapen dawn
With vacant gloaming, sad as half-lit minds,
The weak-limned hour when sick men's sighs are
    drained.
And while I wondered on their being withdrawn,
Gagged by the smothering wing which none unbinds,
I dreaded even a heaven with doors so chained.

Apologia pro Poemate Meo

I, too, saw God through mud —
    The mud that cracked on cheeks when wretches
      smiled.
    War brought more glory to their eyes than blood,
    And gave their laughs more glee than shakes a child.

Merry it was to laugh there —
    Where death becomes absurd and life absurder.
    For power was on us as we slashed bones bare
    Not to feel sickness or remorse of murder.

I, too, have dropped off fear —
    Behind the barrage, dead as my platoon,
    And sailed my spirit surging, light and clear
    Past the entanglement where hopes lay strewn;

And witnessed exultation —
    Faces that used to curse me, scowl for scowl,
    Shine and lift up with passion of oblation,
    Seraphic for an hour; though they were foul.

I have made fellowships —
    Untold of happy lovers in old song.
    For love is not the binding of fair lips
    With the soft silk of eyes that look and long,

By Joy, whose ribbon slips, —
    But wound with war's hard wire whose stakes are
      strong;
    Bound with the bandage of the arm that drips;
    Knit in the welding of the rifle-thong.

I have perceived much beauty
   In the hoarse oaths that kept our courage straight;
   Heard music in the silentness of duty;
   Found peace where shell-storms spouted reddest
     spate.

Nevertheless, except you share
   With them in hell the sorrowful dark of hell,
   Whose world is but the trembling of a flare,
   And heaven but as the highway for a shell,

You shall not hear their mirth:
   You shall not come to think them well content
   By any jest of mine. These men are worth
   Your tears: You are not worth their merriment.

Hospital Barge at Cérisy

Budging the sluggard ripples of the Somme
A barge round old Cérisy slowly slewed.
Softly her engines down the current screwed,
And chuckled softly with contented hum,
Till fairy tinklings struck their crooning dumb.
The waters rumpling at the stern subdued:
The lock-gate took her bulging amplitude:
Gently from out the gurgling lock she swum.

One reading by that calm bank shaded eyes
To watch her lessening westward quietly.
Then, as she neared the bend, her funnel screamed.
And in that long lamentation made him wise
How unto Avilon in agony
Kings passed in the dark barge which Merlin dreamed.

Sonnet

To a Child

Sweet is your antique body, not yet young;
Beauty withheld from youth that looks for youth;
Fair only for your father. Dear among
Masters in art. To all men else uncouth;
Save me, who know your smile comes very old,
Learnt of the happy dead that laughed with gods;
For earlier suns than ours have lent you gold;
Sly fauns and trees have given you jigs and nods.

But soon your heart, hot-beating like a bird's,
Shall slow down. Youth shall lop your hair;
And you must learn wry meanings in our words.
Your smile shall dull, because too keen aware;
And when for hopes your hand shall be uncurled,
Your eyes shall close, being open to the world.

At a Calvary near the Ancre

One ever hangs where shelled roads part.
  In this war He too lost a limb,
But His disciples hide apart;
  And now the Soldiers bear with Him.

Near Golgotha strolls many a priest,
  And in their faces there is pride
That they were flesh-marked by the Beast
  By whom the gentle Christ's denied.

The scribes on all the people shove
  And brawl allegiance to the state,
But they who love the greater love
  Lay down their life; they do not hate.

Miners

There was a whispering in my hearth,
  A sigh of the coal,
Grown wistful of a former earth
  It might recall.

I listened for a tale of leaves
  And smothered ferns,
Frond-forests, and the low sly lives
  Before the fawns.

My fire might show steam-phantoms simmer
  From Time's old cauldron,
Before the birds made nests in summer,
  Or men had children.

But the coals were murmuring of their mine,
  And moans down there
Of boys that slept wry sleep, and men
  Writhing for air.

I saw white bones in the cinder-shard,
  Bones without number.
For many hearts with coal are charred,
  And few remember.

I thought of all that worked dark pits
  Of war, and died
Digging the rock where Death reputes
  Peace lies indeed:

Comforted years will sit soft-chaired,
  In rooms of amber,
The years will stretch their hands, well-cheered
  By our life's ember;

The centuries will burn rich loads
  With which we groaned,
Whose warmth shall lull their dreaming lids,
  While songs are crooned;
But they will not dream of us poor lads,
  Lost in the ground.

Conscious

His fingers wake, and flutter up the bed.
His eyes come open with a pull of will,
Helped by the yellow may-flowers by his head.
A blind-cord drawls across the window-sill . . .
How smooth the floor of the ward is! what a rug!
And who's that talking, somewhere out of sight?
Why are they laughing? What's inside that jug?
'Nurse! Doctor!' 'Yes; all right, all right.'

But sudden dusk bewilders all the air –
There seems no time to want a drink of water.
Nurse looks so far away. And everywhere
Music and roses burnt through crimson slaughter.
Cold; cold; he's cold; and yet so hot:
And there's no light to see the voices by –
No time to dream, and ask – he knows not what.

Dulce Et Decorum Est

Bent double, like old beggars under sacks,
Knock-kneed, coughing like hags, we cursed through
   sludge,
Till on the haunting flares we turned our backs,
And towards our distant rest began to trudge.
Men marched asleep. Many had lost their boots,
But limped on, blood-shod. All went lame, all blind;
Drunk with fatigue; deaf even to the hoots
Of gas-shells dropping softly behind.

Gas! GAS! Quick, boys! – An ecstasy of fumbling
Fitting the clumsy helmets just in time,
But someone still was yelling out and stumbling
And flound'ring like a man in fire or lime. –
Dim through the misty panes and thick green light,
As under a green sea, I saw him drowning.

In all my dreams before my helpless sight
He plunges at me, guttering, choking, drowning.

If in some smothering dreams, you too could pace
Behind the wagon that we flung him in,
And watch the white eyes writhing in his face,
His hanging face, like a devil's sick of sin,
If you could hear, at every jolt, the blood
Come gargling from the froth-corrupted lungs
Bitten as the cud
Of vile, incurable sores on innocent tongues, –
My friend, you would not tell with such high zest
To children ardent for some desperate glory,
The old Lie: *Dulce et decorum est*
Pro patria mori.

The Dead-Beat

He dropped, – more sullenly than wearily,
Lay stupid like a cod, heavy like meat,
And none of us could kick him to his feet;
Just blinked at my revolver, blearily;
– Didn't appear to know a war was on,
Or see the blasted trench at which he stared.
'I'll do 'em in,' he whined, 'If this hand's spared,
I'll murder them, I will.'

                  A low voice said,
'It's Blighty, p'raps, he sees; his pluck's all gone,
Dreaming of all the valiant, that *aren't* dead:
Bold uncles, smiling ministerially;
Maybe his brave young wife, getting her fun
In some new home, improved materially.
It's not these stiffs have crazed him; nor the Hun.'

We sent him down at last, out of the way.
Unwounded; – stout lad, too, before that strafe.
Malingering? Stretcher-bearers winked, 'Not half!'

Next day I heard the Doc's well-whiskied laugh:
'That scum you sent last night soon died. Hooray!'

Insensibility

I

Happy are men who yet before they are killed
Can let their veins run cold.
Whom no compassion fleers
Or makes their feet
Sore on the alleys cobbled with their brothers.
The front line withers,
But they are troops who fade, not flowers
For poets' tearful fooling:
Men, gaps for filling
Losses who might have fought
Longer; but no one bothers.

II

And some cease feeling
Even themselves or for themselves.
Dullness best solves
The tease and doubt of shelling,
And Chance's strange arithmetic
Comes simpler than the reckoning of their shilling.
They keep no check on Armies' decimation.

III

Happy are these who lose imagination:
They have enough to carry with ammunition.
Their spirit drags no pack.
Their old wounds save with cold can not more ache.
Having seen all things red,
Their eyes are rid

Of the hurt of the colour of blood for ever.
And terror's first constriction over,
Their hearts remain small drawn.
Their senses in some scorching cautery of battle
Now long since ironed,
Can laugh among the dying, unconcerned.

IV

Happy the soldier home, with not a notion
How somewhere, every dawn, some men attack,
And many sighs are drained.
Happy the lad whose mind was never trained:
His days are worth forgetting more than not.
He sings along the march
Which we march taciturn, because of dusk,
The long, forlorn, relentless trend
From larger day to huger night.

V

We wise, who with a thought besmirch
Blood over all our soul,
How should we see our task
But through his blunt and lashless eyes?
Alive, he is not vital overmuch;
Dying, not mortal overmuch;
Nor sad, nor proud,
Nor curious at all.
He cannot tell
Old men's placidity from his.

VI

But cursed are dullards whom no cannon stuns,
That they should be as stones.
Wretched are they, and mean
With paucity that never was simplicity.
By choice they made themselves immune
To pity and whatever mourns in man
Before the last sea and the hapless stars;
Whatever mourns when many leave these shores;
Whatever shares
The eternal reciprocity of tears.

Strange Meeting

It seemed that out of the battle I escaped
Down some profound dull tunnel, long since scooped
Through granites which Titanic wars had groined.
Yet also there encumbered sleepers groaned,
Too fast in thought or death to be bestirred.
Then, as I probed them, one sprang up, and stared
With piteous recognition in fixed eyes,
Lifting distressful hands as if to bless.
And by his smile, I knew that sullen hall;
With a thousand fears that vision's face was grained;
Yet no blood reached there from the upper ground,
And no guns thumped, or down the flues made moan.
'Strange, friend,' I said, 'Here is no cause to mourn.'
'None,' said the other, 'Save the undone years,
The hopelessness. Whatever hope is yours,
Was my life also; I went hunting wild
After the wildest beauty in the world,
Which lies not calm in eyes, or braided hair,
But mocks the steady running of the hour,
And if it grieves, grieves richlier than here.
For by my glee might many men have laughed,
And of my weeping something has been left,
Which must die now. I mean the truth untold,
The pity of war, the pity war distilled.
Now men will go content with what we spoiled.
Or, discontent, boil bloody, and be spilled.
They will be swift with swiftness of the tigress,
None will break ranks, though nations trek from
    progress.
Courage was mine, and I had mystery;
Wisdom was mine, and I had mastery;

To miss the march of this retreating world
Into vain citadels that are not walled.
Then, when much blood had clogged their chariot-
    wheels
I would go up and wash them from sweet wells,
Even with truths that lie too deep for taint.
I would have poured my spirit without stint
But not through wounds; not on the cess of war.
Foreheads of men have bled where no wounds were.
I am the enemy you killed, my friend.
I knew you in this dark; for so you frowned
Yesterday through me as you jabbed and killed.
I parried; but my hands were loath and cold.
Let us sleep now . . .'

Asleep

Under his helmet, up against his pack,
After so many days of work and waking
Sleep took him by the brow and laid him back.

There, in the happy no-time of his sleeping,
Death took him by the heart. There heaved a quaking
Of frustrate life, like child within him leaping . . .
Then chest and sleepy arms once more fell slack.

And soon the slow stray blood comes creeping
From the intrusive lead, like ants on track.

*   *   *   *

Whether his deeper sleep lie shaded by the shaking
Of great wings, and the thoughts of stars,
High-pillowed on calm clouds of God's making,
Above these clouds, these rains, these sleets of lead,
And these winds' scimitars;
– Or whether yet his thin and sodden head
Confuses more and more with the low mould,
His hair being one with the grey grass
Of finished fields, and wire-scrags rusty-old, . . .
Who knows? Who hopes? Who troubles? Let it pass!
He sleeps. He sleeps less tremulous, less cold
Than we who wake, and waking say, Alas!

Arms and the Boy

Let the boy try along this bayonet-blade
How cold steel is, and keen with hunger of blood;
Blue with all malice, like a madman's flash;
And thinly drawn with famishing for flesh.

Lend him to stroke these blind, blunt bullet-heads
Which long to nuzzle in the hearts of lads,
Or give him cartridges of fine zinc teeth,
Sharp with the sharpness of grief and death.

For his teeth seem for laughing round an apple.
There lurk no claws behind his fingers supple;
And God will grow no talons at his heels,
Nor antlers through the thickness of his curls.

The Show

My soul looked down from a vague height with Death,
As unremembering how I rose or why,
And saw a sad land, weak with sweats of dearth,
Gray, cratered like the moon with hollow woe,
And fitted with great pocks and scabs of plaques.

Across its beard, that horror of harsh wire,
There moved thin caterpillars, slowly uncoiled.
It seemed they pushed themselves to be as plugs
Of ditches, where they writhed and shrivelled, killed.

By them had slimy paths been trailed and scraped
Round myriad warts that might be little hills.

From gloom's last dregs these long-strung creatures
      crept,
And vanished out of dawn down hidden holes.

(And smell came up from those foul openings
As out of mouths, or deep wounds deepening.)

On dithering feet upgathered, more and more,
Brown strings towards strings of gray, with bristling
      spines,
All migrants from green fields, intent on mire.

Those that were gray, of more abundant spawns,
Ramped on the rest and ate them and were eaten.

I saw their bitten backs curve, loop, and straighten,
I watched those agonies curl, lift, and flatten.

Whereat, in terror what that sight might mean,
I reeled and shivered earthward like a feather.

And Death fell with me, like a deepening moan.

And He, picking a manner of worm, which half had
   hid
Its bruises in the earth, but crawled no further,
Showed me its feet, the feet of many men,
And the fresh-severed head of it, my head.

Futility

Move him into the sun —
Gently its touch awoke him once,
At home, whispering of fields unsown.
Always it woke him, even in France,
Until this morning and this snow.
If anything might rouse him now
The kind old sun will know.

Think how it wakes the seeds —
Woke, once, the clays of a cold star.
Are limbs so dear-achieved, are sides
Full-nerved, — still warm, — too hard to stir?
Was it for this the clay grew tall?
— O what made fatuous sunbeams toil
To break earth's sleep at all?

The End

After the blast of lightning from the east,
The flourish of loud clouds, the Chariot throne,
After the drums of time have rolled and ceased
And from the bronze west long retreat is blown,

Shall Life renew these bodies? Of a truth
All death will he annul, all tears assuage?
Or fill these void veins full again with youth
And wash with an immortal water age?

When I do ask white Age, he saith not so, –
'My head hangs weighed with snow.'
And when I hearken to the Earth she saith
'My fiery heart sinks aching. It is death.
Mine ancient scars shall not be glorified
Nor my titanic tears the seas be dried.'

S.I.W.

I will to the King,
And offer him consolation in his trouble,
For that man there has set his teeth to die,
And being one that hates obedience,
Discipline, and orderliness of life,
I cannot mourn him.

    W. B. YEATS

Patting goodbye, doubtless they told the lad
He'd always show the Hun a brave man's face;
Father would sooner him dead than in disgrace, –
Was proud to see him going, aye, and glad.
Perhaps his Mother whimpered how she'd fret
Until he got a nice, safe wound to nurse.
Sisters would wish girls too could shoot, charge,
    curse, . . .
Brothers – would send his favourite cigarette,
Each week, month after month, they wrote the same,
Thinking him sheltered in some Y.M. Hut,
Where once an hour a bullet missed its aim
And misses teased the hunger of his brain.
His eyes grew old with wincing, and his hand
Reckless with ague. Courage leaked, as sand
From the best sandbags after years of rain.
But never leave, wound, fever, trench-foot, shock,
Untrapped the wretch. And death seemed still withheld
For torture of lying machinally shelled,
At the pleasure of this world's Powers who'd run
    amok.

He'd seen men shoot their hands, on night patrol,
Their people never knew. Yet they were vile.
'Death sooner than dishonour, that's the style!'
So Father said.

                    One dawn, our wire patrol
Carried him. This time, Death had not missed.
We could do nothing, but wipe his bleeding cough.
Could it be accident? – Rifles go off . . .
Not sniped? No. (Later they found the English ball.)

It was the reasoned crisis of his soul.
Against the fires that would not burn him whole
But kept him for death's perjury and scoff
And life's half-promising, and both their riling.

With him they buried the muzzle his teeth had kissed,
And truthfully wrote the Mother 'Tim died smiling.'

And I Must Go

Gongs hum and buzz like saucepan-lid at dusk,
I see a food-hog whet his gold-filled tusk
To eat less bread, and more luxurious rusk.

Then sometimes late at night my window bumps
From gunnery-practice, till my small heart thumps
And listens for the shell-shrieks and the crumps,
                    But that's not all.

For leaning out last midnight on my sill
I heard the sighs of men, that have no skill
To speak of their distress, no, nor the will!
                    A voice I know. And I must go.

The Next War

War's a joke for me and you,
When we know such dreams are true.
   SASSOON

Out there, we've walked quite friendly up to Death;
  Sat down and eaten with him, cool and bland, –
  Pardoned his spilling mess-tins in our hand.
We've sniffed the green thick odour of his breath, –
Our eyes wept, but our courage didn't writhe.
  He's spat at us with bullets and he's coughed
  Shrapnel. We chorused when he sang aloft;
We whistled while he shaved us with his scythe.

Oh, Death was never enemy of ours!
  We laughed at him, we leagued with him, old chum.
No soldier's paid to kick against his powers.
  We laughed, knowing that better men would come,
And greater wars: when each proud fighter brags
He wars on Death – for Life; not men – for flags.

Greater Love

Red lips are not so red
　As the stained stones kissed by the English dead.
Kindness of wooed and wooer
Seems shame to their love pure.
O Love, your eyes lose lure
　When I behold eyes blinded in my stead!

Your slender attitude
　Trembles not exquisite like limbs knife-skewed,
Rolling and rolling there
Where God seems not to care;
Till the fierce Love they bear
　Cramps them in death's extreme decrepitude.

Your voice sings not so soft, –
　Though even as wind murmuring through raftered
　　loft, –
Your dear voice is not dear,
Gentle, and evening clear,
As theirs whom none now hear
　Now earth has stopped their piteous mouths that
　　coughed.

Heart, you were never hot,
　Nor large, nor full like hearts made great with shot;
And though your hand be pale,
Paler are all which trail
Your cross through flame and hail:
　Weep, you may weep, for you may touch them not.

Mental Cases

Who are these? Why sit they here in twilight?
Wherefore rock they, purgatorial shadows,
Drooping tongues from jaws that slob their relish,
Baring teeth that leer like skulls' tongues wicked?
Stroke on stroke of pain, – but what slow panic,
Gouged these chasms round their fretted sockets?
Ever from their hair and through their hand palms
Misery swelters. Surely we have perished
Sleeping, and walk hell; but who these hellish?

– These are men whose minds the Dead have ravished.
Memory fingers in their hair of murders,
Multitudinous murders they once witnessed.
Wading sloughs of flesh these helpless wander,
Treading blood from lungs that had loved laughter.
Always they must see these things and hear them,
Batter of guns and shatter of flying muscles,
Carnage incomparable and human squander
Rucked too thick for these men's extrication.

Therefore still their eyeballs shrink tormented
Back into their brains, because on their sense
Sunlight seems a bloodsmear; night comes blood-black;
Dawn breaks open like a wound that bleeds afresh
– Thus their heads wear this hilarious, hideous,
Awful falseness of set-smiling corpses.
– Thus their hands are plucking at each other;
Picking at the rope-knouts of their scourging;
Snatching after us who smote them, brother,
Pawing us who dealt them war and madness.

The Send-off

Down the close, darkening lanes they sang their way
To the siding-shed,
And lined the train with faces grimly gay.

Their breasts were stuck all white with wreath and
    spray
As men's are, dead.

Dull porters watched them, and a casual tramp
Stood staring hard,
Sorry to miss them from the upland camp.
Then, unmoved, signals nodded, and a lamp
Winked to the guard.

So secretly, like wrongs hushed-up, they went.
They were not ours:
We never heard to which front these were sent.

Nor there if they yet mock what women meant
Who gave them flowers.

Shall they return to beatings of great bells
In wild trainloads?
A few, a few, too few for drums and yells,
May creep back, silent, to still village wells
Up half-known roads.

Parable of the Old Men and the Young

So Abram rose, and clave the wood, and went,
And took the fire with him, and a knife.
And as they sojourned both of them together,
Isaac the first-born spake and said, My Father,
Behold the preparations, fire and iron,
But where the lamb for this burnt-offering?
Then Abram bound the youth with belts and straps,
And builded parapets and trenches there,
And stretchèd forth the knife to slay his son.
When lo! an angel called him out of heaven,
Saying, Lay not thy hand upon the lad,
Neither do anything to him. Behold,
A ram caught in a thicket by its horns;
Offer the Ram of Pride instead of him.
But the old man would not so, but slew his son
And half the seed of Europe, one by one.

Disabled

He sat in a wheeled chair, waiting for dark,
And shivered in his ghastly suit of grey,
Legless, sewn short at elbow. Through the park
Voices of boys rang saddening like a hymn,
Voices of play and pleasure after day,
Till gathering sleep had mothered them from him.

About this time Town used to swing so gay
When glow-lamps budded in the light-blue trees
And girls glanced lovelier as the air grew dim,
– In the old times, before he threw away his knees.
Now he will never feel again how slim
Girls' waists are, or how warm their subtle hands,
All of them touch him like some queer disease.

There was an artist silly for his face,
For it was younger than his youth, last year.
Now he is old; his back will never brace;
He's lost his colour very far from here,
Poured it down shell-holes till the veins ran dry,
And half his lifetime lapsed in the hot race,
And leap of purple spurted from his thigh.
One time he liked a bloodsmear down his leg,
After the matches carried shoulder-high.
It was after football, when he'd drunk a peg,
He thought he'd better join. He wonders why . . .
Someone had said he'd look a god in kilts.

That's why; and maybe, too, to please his Meg,
Aye, that was it, to please the giddy jilts,
He asked to join. He didn't have to beg;

Smiling they wrote his lie; aged nineteen years.
Germans he scarcely thought of; and no fears
Of Fear came yet. He thought of jewelled hilts
For daggers in plaid socks; of smart salutes;
And care of arms; and leave; and pay arrears;
Esprit de corps; and hints for young recruits.
And soon, he was drafted out with drums and cheers.

Some cheered him home, but not as crowds cheer
  Goal.
Only a solemn man who brought him fruits
Thanked him; and then inquired about his soul.
Now, he will spend a few sick years in Institutes,
And do what things the rules consider wise,
And take whatever pity they may dole.
Tonight he noticed how the women's eyes
Passed from him to the strong men that were whole.
How cold and late it is! Why don't they come
And put him into bed? Why don't they come?

A Terre

(Being the philosophy of many Soldiers)

Sit on the bed; I'm blind, and three parts shell,
Be careful; can't shake hands now; never shall.
Both arms have mutinied against me — brutes.
My fingers fidget like ten idle brats.

I tried to peg out soldierly — no use!
One dies of war like any old disease.
This bandage feels like pennies on my eyes.
I have my medals? — Discs to make eyes close.
My glorious ribbons? — Ripped from my own back
In scarlet shreds. (That's for your poetry book.)

A short life and a merry one, my brick!
We used to say we'd hate to live dead old, —
Yet now . . . I'd willingly be puffy, bald,
And patriotic. Buffers catch from boys
At least the jokes hurled at them. I suppose
Little I'd ever teach a son, but hitting,
Shooting, war, hunting, all the arts of hurting.
Well, that's what I learnt, — that, and making money.
Your fifty years ahead seem none too many?
Tell me how long I've got? God! For one year
To help myself to nothing more than air!
One Spring! Is one too good to spare, too long?
Spring wind would work its own way to my lung,
And grow me legs as quick as lilac-shoots.
My servant's lamed, but listen how he shouts!
When I'm lugged out, he'll still be good for that.
Here in this mummy-case, you know, I've thought

How well I might have swept his floors for ever,
I'd ask no night off when the bustle's over,
Enjoying so the dirt. Who's prejudiced
Against a grimed hand when his own's quite dust,
Less live than specks that in the sun-shafts turn,
Less warm than dust that mixes with arms' tan?
I'd love to be a sweep, now, black as Town,
Yes, or a muckman. Must I be his load?
O Life, Life, let me breathe, – a dug-out rat!
Not worse than ours the existences rats lead –
Nosing along at night down some safe vat,
They find a shell-proof home before they rot.
Dead men may envy living mites in cheese,
Or good germs even. Microbes have their joys,
And subdivide, and never come to death,
Certainly flowers have the easiest time on earth.
'I shall be one with nature, herb, and stone.'
Shelley would tell me. Shelley would be stunned;
The dullest Tommy hugs that fancy now.
'Pushing up daisies,' is their creed, you know.
To grain, then, go my fat, to buds my sap,
For all the usefulness there is in soap.
D'you think the Boche will ever stew man-soup?
Some day, no doubt, if . . .
                              Friend, be very sure
I shall be better off with plants that share
More peaceably the meadow and the shower.
Soft rains will touch me, – as they could touch once,
And nothing but the sun shall make me ware.
Your guns may crash around me. I'll not hear;
Or, if I wince, I shall not know I wince.
Don't take my soul's poor comfort for your jest.
Soldiers may grow a soul when turned to fronds,
But here the thing's best left at home with friends.

My soul's a little grief, grappling your chest,
To climb your throat on sobs; easily chased
On other sighs and wiped by fresher winds.

Carry my crying spirit till it's weaned
To do without what blood remained these wounds.

The Kind Ghosts

She sleeps on soft, last breaths; but no ghost looms
Out of the stillness of her palace wall,
Her wall of boys on boys and dooms on dooms.

She dreams of golden gardens and sweet glooms,
Not marvelling why her roses never fall
Nor what red mouths were torn to make their blooms.

The shades keep down which well might roam her
    hall.
Quiet their blood lies in her crimson rooms
And she is not afraid of their footfall.

They move not from her tapestries, their pall,
Nor pace her terraces, their hecatombs,
Lest aught she be disturbed, or grieved at all.

Shadwell Stair

I am the ghost of Shadwell Stair.
  Along the wharves by the water-house,
  And through the cavernous slaughter-house,
I am the shadow that walks there.

Yet I have flesh both firm and cool,
  And eyes tumultuous as the gems
  Of moons and lamps in the lapping Thames
When dusk sails wavering down the pool.

Shuddering the purple street-arc burns
  Where I watch always; from the banks
  Dolorously the shipping clanks,
And after me a strange tide turns.

I walk till the stars of London wane
  And dawn creeps up the Shadwell Stair.
  But when the crowing syrens blare
I with another ghost am lain.

Exposure

I

Our brains ache, in the merciless iced east winds that
   knife us . . .
Wearied we keep awake because the night is silent . . .
Low drooping flares confuse our memory of the
   salient . . .
Worried by silence, sentries whisper, curious, nervous,
        But nothing happens.

Watching, we hear the mad gusts tugging on the wire.
Like twitching agonies of men among its brambles.
Northward incessantly, the flickering gunnery rumbles,
Far off, like a dull rumour of some other war.
        What are we doing here?

The poignant misery of dawn begins to grow . . .
We only know war lasts, rain soaks, and clouds sag
   stormy.
Dawn massing in the east her melancholy army
Attacks once more in ranks on shivering ranks of gray,
        But nothing happens.

Sudden successive flights of bullets streak the silence.
Less deadly than the air that shudders black with snow,
With sidelong flowing flakes that flock, pause and
   renew,
We watch them wandering up and down the wind's
   nonchalance,
        But nothing happens.

Pale flakes with lingering stealth come feeling for our
    faces –
We cringe in holes, back on forgotten dreams, and
    stare, snow-dazed,
Deep into grassier ditches. So we drowse, sun-dozed,
Littered with blossoms trickling where the blackbird
    fusses.
           Is it that we are dying?

Slowly our ghosts drag home: glimpsing the sunk fires
    glozed
With crusted dark-red jewels; crickets jingle there;
For hours the innocent mice rejoice: the house is
    theirs;
Shutters and doors all closed: on us the doors are
    closed –
           We turn back to our dying.

Since we believe not otherwise can kind fires burn;
Now ever suns smile true on child, or field, or fruit.
For God's invincible spring our love is made afraid;
Therefore, not loath, we lie out here; therefore were
    born,
           For love of God seems dying.

Tonight, His frost will fasten on this mud and us,
Shrivelling many hands and puckering foreheads crisp.
The burying-party, picks and shovels in their shaking
    grasp,
Pause over half-known faces. All their eyes are ice,
           But nothing happens.

The Sentry

We'd found an old Boche dug-out, and he knew,
And gave us hell, for shell on frantic shell
Hammered on top, but never quite burst through.
Rain, guttering down in waterfalls of slime
Kept slush waist high, that rising hour by hour,
Choked up the steps too thick with clay to climb.
What murk of air remained stank old, and sour
With fumes of whizz-bangs, and the smell of men
Who'd lived there years, and left their curse in the
    den,
If not their corpses. . . .
                          There we herded from the blast
Of whizz-bangs, but one found our door at last.
Buffeting eyes and breath, snuffing the candles.
And thud! flump! thud! down the steep steps came
    thumping
And splashing in the flood, deluging muck –
The sentry's body; then his rifle, handles
Of old Boche bombs, and mud in ruck on ruck.
We dredged him up, for killed, until he whined
'O sir, my eyes – I'm blind – I'm blind, I'm blind!'
Coaxing, I held a flame against his lids
And said if he could see the least blurred light
He was not blind; in time he'd get all right.
'I can't,' he sobbed. Eyeballs, huge-bulged like squids
Watch my dreams still; but I forgot him there
In posting next for duty, and sending a scout
To beg a stretcher somewhere, and floundering about
To other posts under the shrieking air.

Those other wretches, how they bled and spewed,
And one who would have drowned himself for good, —
I try not to remember these things now.
Let dread hark back for one word only: how
Half-listening to that sentry's moans and jumps,
And the wild chattering of his broken teeth,
Renewed most horribly whenever crumps
Pummelled the roof and slogged the air beneath —
Through the dense din, I say, we heard him shout
'I see your lights!' But ours had long died out.

Smile, Smile, Smile

Head to limp head, the sunk-eyed wounded scanned
Yesterday's Mail; the casualties (typed small)
And (large) Vast Booty from our Latest Haul.
Also, they read of Cheap Homes, not yet planned;
For, said the paper, 'When this war is done
The men's first instinct will be making homes.
Meanwhile their foremost need is aerodromes,
It being certain war has just begun.
Peace would do wrong to our undying dead, —
The sons we offered might regret they died
If we got nothing lasting in their stead.
We must be solidly indemnified.
Though all be worthy Victory which all bought,
We rulers sitting in this ancient spot
Would wrong our very selves if we forgot
The greatest glory will be theirs who fought,
Who kept this nation in integrity.
Nation? — The half-limbed readers did not chafe
But smiled at one another curiously
Like secret men who know their secret safe.
This is the thing they know and never speak,
That England one by one had fled to France
(Not many elsewhere now save under France).
Pictures of these broad smiles appear each week,
And people in whose voice real feeling rings
Say: How they smile! They're happy now, poor things.

Spring Offensive

Halted against the shade of a last hill,
They fed, and, lying easy, were at ease
And, finding comfortable chests and knees
Carelessly slept. But many there stood still
To face the stark, blank sky beyond the ridge,
Knowing their feet had come to the end of the world.

Marvelling they stood, and watched the long grass
  swirled
By the May breeze, murmurous with wasp and midge,
For though the summer oozed into their veins
Like the injected drug for their bones' pains,
Sharp on their souls hung the imminent line of grass,
Fearfully flashed the sky's mysterious glass.

Hour after hour they ponder the warm field –
And the far valley behind, where the buttercups
Had blessed with gold their slow boots coming up,
Where even the little brambles would not yield,
But clutched and clung to them like sorrowing hands;
They breathe like trees unstirred.

Till like a cold gust thrilled the little word
At which each body and its soul begird
And tighten them for battle. No alarms
Of bugles, no high flags, no clamorous haste –
Only a lift and flare of eyes that faced
The sun, like a friend with whom their love is done.
O larger shone that smile against the sun, –
Mightier than his whose bounty these have spurned.

So, soon they topped the hill, and raced together
Over an open stretch of herb and heather
Exposed. And instantly the whole sky burned
With fury against them; and soft sudden cups
Opened in thousands for their blood; and the green
  slopes
Chasmed and steepened sheer to infinite space.

Of them who running on that last high place
Leapt to swift unseen bullets, or went up
On the hot blast and fury of hell's upsurge,
Or plunged and fell away past this world's verge,
Some say God caught them even before they fell.

But what say such as from existence' brink
Ventured but drave too swift to sink.
The few who rushed in the body to enter hell,
And there out-fiending all its fiends and flames
With superhuman inhumanities,
Long-famous glories, immemorial shames –
And crawling slowly back, have by degrees
Regained cool peaceful air in wonder –
Why speak they not of comrades that went under?

Chronology of Brooke's and Owen's Lives

Year	Ages	Lives
1887		Rupert Chawner Brooke born 3 August in Rugby; second of three sons of William Parker Brooke, a housemaster at Rugby School, and Mary Cotterill
1893		Wilfred Edward Salter Owen born in Plas Wilmot, Oswestry; eldest of four children of Tom Owen, a railway official, and Susan Shaw
1897	10	Brooke attends Hillbrow Preparatory School, Rugby
	4	Owen family move to Birkenhead
1900	7	Owen attends Birkenhead Institute
1901	14	Brooke attends Rugby School as member of his father's house
1906	19	Brooke wins scholarship to read Classics at King's College, Cambridge
1907	20	Brooke begins to publish poems
1908	21	Brooke becomes friends with Edward Marsh
	15	Owen family move to Shrewsbury. Owen attends Shrewsbury Technical School
1909	22	Brooke becomes President of the Cambridge University Fabian Society. Awarded a Second in his Classical Tripos and so switches to English Literature for his final year
1910	23	Brooke spends summer touring south-west speaking on Poor Law reform on behalf of Fabians. Moves to Old Vicarage, Grantchester in December
1911	24	Brooke travels on continent for five months, staying in Munich and Florence. *Poems* published in December
	18	Owen works as a pupil-teacher at Wyle Cop School, Shrewsbury, whilst studying for University of London matriculation exam. Fails to matriculate and takes unpaid position as lay assistant and pupil of the Reverend Herbert Wigan at Dunsden, an evangelical parish near Reading
1912	25	Brooke suffers nervous breakdown and convalesces in Cannes and Munich. Returns to Germany for

Chronology of Their Times

Year	Literary Context	Historical Events
1887	Conan Doyle, *A Study in Scarlet*	Queen Victoria's Golden Jubilee
1893	John Davidson, *Fleet Street Eclogues* Francis Thompson, *Poems*	Independent Labour Party formed
1897	James, *What Maisie Knew* Stoker, *Dracula*	Queen Victoria's Diamond Jubilee; Revolt on Indian North-West Frontier
1900	Death of John Ruskin	Boxer Rebellion in China
1901	Kipling, *Kim*	Death of Queen Victoria and accession of Edward VII
1906	Galsworthy, *The Man of Property*	First Labour MPs
1908	Chesterton, *The Man Who Was Thursday* Hardy, *The Dynasts*	
1909	Death of Swinburne Forster, *Howards End*	Old Age Pension introduced; Blériot flies across English Channel
1910	Yeats, *Responsibilities and Other Poems*	Death of Edward VII and accession of George V; Post-Impressionist exhibition in London
1911	Masefield, *The Everlasting Mercy*	Amundsen reaches South Pole
1912	*Georgian Poetry 1911–1912* de la Mare, *The Listeners*	Loss of the Titanic

Year	Ages	Lives
		two months in April and lives in Berlin. Conceives *Georgian Poetry* with Edward Marsh, Harold Monro and Wilfrid Gibson
1913	26	Brooke awarded Fellowship at King's. Travels to America in May and explores America and Canada before moving on to Samoa and Fiji. Spends December in New Zealand
	20	Owen abandons evangelical religion and leaves Dunsden suffering from physical and mental illness. Fails scholarship exam for University College, Reading and moves to Bordeaux in September to teach English at Berlitz School
1914	27	Brooke spends four months in Tahiti, returning to England in June. Commissioned in the Royal Naval Division in September and takes part in unsuccessful Antwerp expedition. Joins Hood Battalion at Blandford for training in December
	21	Owen becomes tutor to the Léger family in the High Pyrenees. Returns to Bordeaux in September to become freelance English teacher. Accepts post as private tutor to the de la Touche family at Mérignac in December
1915	27	Hood Battalion sail for the Dardanelles in February. Brooke contracts acute septicaemia from a mosquito bite and dies at Scyros on 23 April. *1914 and Other Poems* published in June
	22	Owen returns to England in September and enlists in Artists' Rifles.
1916	23	Owen commissioned as Second Lieutenant in Manchester Regiment in June. Arrives in France on 29 December
1917	24	Owen joins Manchester Regiment on Somme front. Evacuated to 13th Casualty Clearing Station at Gailly in March with concussion and again in May with shell-shock. Returns to England and is sent to Craiglockhart War Hospital for treatment. Begins friendship with Siegfried Sassoon. Passed fit for home service by Medical Board in October and rejoins Manchester Regiment at Scarborough. Promoted to Lieutenant

Year	Literary Context	Historical Events
1913	*Lawrence, Sons and Lovers*	Panama Canal opens
1914	*Des Imagistes* anthology *Frost, North of Boston*	Outbreak of First World War; Battles of Mons and the Marne
1915	*Buchan, The Thirty-Nine Steps* *Wilfrid Gibson, Battle*	Battle of Neuve Chapelle; Gallipoli campaign; Loss of the *Lusitania*
1916	*Henri Barbusse, Le Feu*	Battles of Verdun and the Somme; Irish revolt
1917	*Sassoon, The Old Huntsman and Other Poems* *Graves, Fairies and Fusiliers* *Laurence Binyon, For the Fallen and Other Poems*	Battle of Passchendaele; Russian Revolution; America enters First World War

Year	Ages	Lives
1918		*Collected Poems of Rupert Brooke. With a Memoir* published
	25	Owen returns to France in August and is awarded Military Cross in October after successful action in Beaurevoir-Fonsomme line. Killed by machine gun fire on Oise-Sambre canal on 4 November
1920		*Poems by Wilfred Owen* published
1928		Revised edition of *Collected Poems of Rupert Brooke: With a Memoir* published
1931		*The Poems of Wilfred Owen: Edited with a Memoir by Edmund Blunden* published

Year	Literary Context	Historical Events
1918	Sassoon, *Counter-Attack and Other Poems* Hopkins, *Poems* Wyndham Lewis, *Tarr*	Battle of Arras; German offensive on Somme: First World War ends
1920	Pound, *Hugh Selwyn Mauberley*	First meeting of League of Nations
1926		The General Strike
1928	Edmund Blunden, *Undertones of War* Sassoon, *Memoirs of a Fox-Hunting Man*	British women win equal voting rights with men
1931	Woolf, *The Waves* Day-Lewis, *From Feathers to Iron*	